1994
/Nineteen Ninety Four

David Simpson & Richard Callaghan

G000058244

MY WORLD PUBLISHING

Designed by **courage**

Text copyright © David Simpson and Richard Callaghan

Design copyright © **courage**

ISBN: 978 1 901888 66 9

First Published 2012

Published in Great Britain by:
My World Publishing
Chase House
Rainton Bridge Business Park
Tyne and Wear
DH4 5RA
Tel: 0191 3055165

www.myworldpublishing.co.uk

*My World Publishing is an imprint of Business Education
Publishers Ltd.*

British Cataloguing-in-Publications Data.
*A catalogue record for this book is available from the British
Library.*

Printed in Great Britain by Ashford Colour Press Ltd.

1994
/Nineteen Ninety Four

HELLO
BOYS.

Unveiled in **1994**, Eva Herzigova's Wonderbra ad propelled her to stardom around the world.

The sensational billboard posters were blamed for stopping traffic and causing accidents as commuters stared at the huge roadside posters!

1994 Number 1 Singles

Chaka Demus and Pliers	/ Twist and Shout / 2 January 1994	
D.Ream	/ Things Can Only Get Better / 16 January 1994	
Mariah Carey	/ Without You / 13 February 1994	
Doop	/ Doop / 13 March 1994	
Take That	/ Everything Changes / 3 April 1994	
Prince	/ The Most Beautiful Girl in the World / 17 April 1994	
Tony Di Bart	/ The Real Thing / 1 May 1994	

Nancy Kerrigan
ATTACKED
On January 6, 1994

American figure skater Nancy Kerrigan was attacked during a practice session for the 1994 U.S. Figure Skating Championships in Detroit. Fortunately, Kerrigan's leg was only bruised, not broken, but she was forced to withdraw from the Championships. The attacker was Shane Stant, who was hired by Jeff Gillooly and Shawn Eckhardt to break Kerrigan's leg, in order to stop her from skating. Gillooly was the ex-husband of American figure skater Tonya Harding, Kerrigan's rival, whilst Eckhardt was her bodyguard. Harding admitted to helping to cover up the attack, pleaded guilty to conspiracy to hinder prosecution, and was fined $100,000 for her part in the affair.

1994 saw Russian Cosmonaut **Valeri Polyakov** set the record for the longest continuous time spent in space by a human being. Polyakov spent 437 days in space aboard the Russian Space Station Mir, making the journey up on **January 8, 1994**, before finally returning to Earth on March 22 1995, a total time of

437 days, 17 hours and 58 minutes

spent in Space. Many scientists took Polyakov's ability to survive and continue to function for such an extended period, as evidence that people would be able to deal with much longer manned spaceflights than previously envisaged, including manned missions to Mars.

TV DEBUTS

New programmes airing on British television for the first time in **1994** included:

Time Team   / Hosted by Tony Robinson
                              / 16 January 1994 / Channel 4

Room 101   / Hosted by Nick Hancock
                              / 4 July 1994 BBC 2

Police Camera Action   / Hosted by Alastair Stewart
                              / 7 September 1994 / ITV

Ready, Steady Cook   / Hosted by Fern Britton
                              / 24 October 1994 / BBC 2

Thanks for the poor security

Who stole our Scream?

On February 12, 1994,

as the world's media descended on Norway for the opening of the Winter Olympics, Oslo's National Gallery became the setting for a high profile theft.

Four men broke into the gallery and made off with *The Scream*, one of a famous series of paintings of that name produced by Norwegian artist Edvard Munch.

The thieves left a cheeky note criticising the gallery's security.

The painting was recovered, undamaged, on May 7, by Norwegian police, assisted by British police agents who specialised in covert operations.

Four men would be charged with the theft in 1996 but would be released on the grounds that the British agents, involved in their capture, had entered Norway under false identities.

In 1994 Heart Management placed the following advert in a magazine called *The Stage*:

WANTED: R.U. 18–23 with the ability to sing/dance? R.U. streetwise, outgoing, ambitious, and dedicated? Heart Management Ltd. are a widely successful music industry management consortium currently forming a choreographed, singing/dancing, all-female pop act for a recording deal. Open audition. Danceworks, 16 Balderton Street. Friday 4 March. 11am-5:30pm. Please bring sheet music or backing cassette.

Following a series of auditions, Melanie Brown, Victoria Adams, Lianne Morgan, Geri Haliwell and Michelle Stephenson were selected. With Morgan replaced by Melanie Chisholm, the group were given the name "Touch". In July, Stephenson was replaced by Emma Bunton and the group was renamed "Spice". In June 1996, they released their first single "Wannabe" as **THE SPICE GIRLS**.

Huge thanks to Don Ku who on **March 8, 1994** was granted a patent for a wheeled suitcase with a collapsible towing handle, without him going on holiday would be so much more ... well heavier!

March 9, 1994

saw Hugh Grant and Richard Curtis become a team for the first time with the release and surprise hit of

FOUR WEDDINGS AND A FUNERAL.

The film, which had a budget of just $4.4m, managed to take more than $245m at the box office and received an Academy Award nomination for Best Picture. The movie's humour, style and performances would make it a firm favourite with both audiences and critics and launch many of its stars to long and successful careers in Hollywood.

THE ORDINATION OF WOMEN

1994 saw the Church of England take an enormous step towards modernity as it ordained its first women priests. On **March 12, 1994**, 32 women were ordained as priests in a service at Bristol Cathedral. The service was officiated by Bishop Barry Rogerson, and the first woman priest in the Church of England was Angela Berners-Wilson.

In March 1994,

APPLE

launched the Power Macintosh, later known as **Power Mac**.

The Macs operated at speeds of up to 110 Mhz.

Apple continued to produce Power Macs until August 2006.

LOCH NESS MONSTER A FAKE

On March 12, 1994, a big game hunter, called Marmaduke Wetherell, revealed that the most famous photograph ever taken of the Loch Ness monster was a hoax set up to dupe *The Daily Mail*.

The photograph, showing the monster's head and neck, appeared in the newspaper in April 1934 where it was claimed it had been taken by London surgeon Robert Kenneth Wilson, who always distanced himself from the photograph.

Wetherell apparently used the services of a sculptor to construct the beast and claimed that he'd simply attributed the photo to the surgeon, to give the image greater credibility.

March 19, 1994

saw the release in Japan of **Super Metroid** for the SNES.

Super Metroid is widely regarded as one of the most influential games ever made, and was critically lauded on its release, meeting with almost universal acclaim. It was the last *Metroid* title for eight years, but its influence was felt throughout the gaming industry, with many of the game's innovative elements becoming commonplace throughout future games.

The 66th
ACADEMY AWARDS

21st March, 1994 Presents...

Best Picture
Schindler's List

Best Director
Steven Spielberg
Schindler's List

Best Actor
Tom Hanks
Philadelphia

Best Actress
Holly Hunter
The Piano

Best Supporting Actor
Tommy Lee Jones
The Fugitive

Best Supporting Actress
Anna Paquin
The Piano

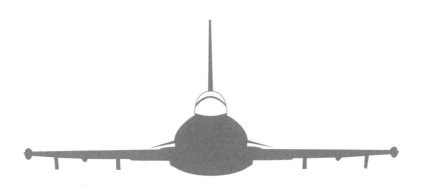

March 27, 1994 saw the first flight of the

EUROFIGHTER,

the first fighter jet built in collaboration between a number of European nations. It was built by the major aerospace companies from Italy, West Germany, Spain and the UK: Alenia Aeronautica, EADS and BAE Systems. The idea had been proposed in the mid-1980s, but it took almost ten years of wrangling and negotiating between the member companies to finally come up with a working plane, the Eurofighter Typhoon. Since then the Eurofighter has entered service in the air forces of the UK, Italy, Germany, Spain, Saudi Arabia and Austria.

KURT COBAIN

The body of rock icon, Kurt Cobain, lead singer of Nirvana was found at his home at Lake Washington, Seattle on **April 8, 1994** after shooting himself in the head.

He had suffered an addiction to a number of substances including heroin and had made several suicide attempts during 1994.

Cobain, aged 27, had been missing since his night time departure from a drug recovery centre in Los Angeles on **March 31, 1994.**

A coroner's report estimated that Cobain had died on **April 5, 1994.** A public vigil attended by 7,000 mourners was held in a park at Seattle Center.

The Rwandan Genocide

1994 saw one of the worst atrocities in recent history as an estimated 800,000 people were killed in the East African country of Rwanda. The genocide took place over a 100 day period from April 6 until the middle of July, having been triggered by the assassination of Rwandan President Juvenal Habyarimana and his Burundian counterpart Cyprien Ntaryamira. This set in motion the massacre of many people of the Tutsi ethnic minority by the majority Hutu people.

SISTINE CHAPEL
RESTORED

On April 8, 1994,

the Sistine Chapel, at the
pope's apostolic palace in
the Vatican City, reopened
following restoration which had
commenced in 1980.

The chapel features work
by the artists Michelangelo,
Pietro Perugino, Sandro Botticelli
and Pinturicchio. The most
famous feature of the chapel is,
of course, the ceiling frescoe by
Michelangelo, depicting the
Last Judgment.

1994 saw the release of Blur's biggest hit, and the album which defined them in the minds of many of the public, *Parklife*. With the singles "Girls and Boys", "End of a Century", "Parklife" and "To The End". *Parklife* gave Blur some of their most recognisable tunes and, debuting at number 1 in the Album charts, remained on the chart for 90 weeks, *Parklife* was Blur's most successful recording to date and one which came to be regarded as the archetypal Britpop record.

....

"All the people. So many people. They all go hand in hand. Hand in hand through their parklife."

....

The Eurovision Song Contest, the Point Theatre, Dublin, **April 30, 1994,** saw the birth of a phenomenon. But it wasn't one of the Eurovision acts which would become a worldwide success, rather it was an act that lasted for seven minutes during the show's interval. That interval saw the debut of RIVERDANCE; Irish dancing which was set to become a massive international hit. It spawned a hit single, which was the top of the Irish charts for 18 weeks, stage shows, and launched Michael Flatley's international career.

AYRTON
SENNA
21 March 1960 - 1 May 1994
(Aged 34)

On Sunday, May 1, 1994

Formula One racing mourned the loss of the
three times World Champion racing driver,
Ayrton Senna.

Senna was killed after his car hit a concrete wall
at 205 mph during the San Marino grand prix
in Italy. Earlier that day, Senna had discussed
the possibility of setting up and leading a new
drivers' safety group.

During the qualifying races that weekend, one
racing driver, Rubens Barrichello, suffered a
broken nose and broken arm on the Friday and
in a separate crash on the Saturday, Austrian
driver Roland Ratzenberger was killed.

Senna's body was flown back to Brazil, his home
nation, where over 200,000 people paid their
respects to his coffin as it lay in state in the
legislative building of Sao Paulo's Ibirapuera Park.

On May 6, 1994, the **Channel Tunnel** opened in a ceremony featuring Her Majesty the Queen and French President, Francoise Mitterrand.

Tunnelling had begun in 1988 after an agreement to build was reached in 1985 between the British and French governments. The tunnels on the British and French sides came together in 1990, but the official opening did not happen until 1994.

On May 6, the Queen travelled by Eurostar to Calais for the first opening ceremony and returned on a French Le Shuttle Train, with Mitterrand, to Folkestone, for an opening ceremony on the English side.

At its peak there were as many as 15,000 people employed in the construction of the tunnel which claimed the lives of ten workers, eight of whom were British.

1994 Number 1 Singles

Stiltskin	/ Inside / 8 May 1994	
Manchester United Football Team	/ Come on You Reds / 15 May 1994	
Wet Wet Wet	/ Love is All Around / 29 May 1994	
Whigfield	/ Saturday Night / 11 September 1994	
Take That	/ Sure / 9 October 1994	
Pato Banton	/ Baby Come Back / 23 October 1994	
Baby D	/ Let Me Be Your Fantasy / 20 November 1994	
East 17	/ Stay Another Day / 4 December 1994	

In 1994 love really was all around ... and around ... and around.

In fact, for 15 weeks, "Love Is All Around" was number one in the UK singles chart.

Released on **May 9, 1994,** Wet Wet Wet's cover of The Troggs' 1967 single became a hit after being featured in *Four Weddings And A Funeral*, that year's surprise British box-office success. It remained in the top 75 for 37 weeks, and in the end it was deleted by Wet Wet Wet, as well as being banned by certain radio stations simply because they'd had enough of it!

NELSON MANDELA ELECTED

May 10, 1994,

four years after he walked free from prison, Nelson Mandela became the first black President of South Africa. Mandela, who had led the African National Congress during negotiations to end Apartheid, saw his party win 62% of the popular vote in South Africa's first democratic multi-racial elections. With F.W. de Klerk as his first deputy and Thabo Mbeki as his second, Mandela set about healing the rifts in South African society, and turning it into a modern African nation.

Blair **Vs.** Brown
The deal.

Granita, a restaurant in London's Islington, was the site of one of the most significant events in modern British political history in **May 1994**. It was there that Tony Blair and Gordon Brown sat to decide who would become the next leader of the Labour Party, following the death of John Smith on the 12th of May. In return for assurances about his position and, some say, his future accession to the leadership, Gordon Brown agreed not to stand for leader of the Labour Party that year, giving Tony Blair an almost unopposed run to the leadership, and ultimately to the office of Prime Minister.

TIGER WOODS' FIRST BIG WIN

1994 was the year that a young golfer from Orange County, California, Eldrick Tont "Tiger" Woods, won his first ever U.S. Amateur Championship, making him at age 18 the youngest person to win the U.S. Amateur at that time. This would not be a flash in the pan, however, with Woods going on to be one of the most successful golfers in the history of the game, an achievement which would make him one of the richest sportsmen on the planet.

Jacqueline Kennedy Onassis

Former First Lady of America, Jacqueline Kennedy
Onassis, known to the world as Jackie O died
peacefully in her sleep in the late evening of
Thursday, May 19, 1994.

She had been suffering from a form of cancer
called Non-Hodgkin's Lymphona diagnosed earlier
in the year.

Born Jacqueline Lee Bouvier on July 28, 1929, she
married John F. Kennedy in 1953 and became First
Lady following his election as U.S. President in
1960. She was famed for her beauty and as a fashion
icon and for the tragic events of November 22, 1963
when she sat in the car with her husband at the time
of his assassination.

In 1968 Jackie married the Greek shipping magnate
Aristotle Onassis who died in 1975. She never
remarried following his death.

What was then Europe's tallest, fastest and steepest rollercoaster opened in 1994.

THE BIG ONE

then known as

THE PEPSI MAX BIG ONE

at Blackpool Pleasure Beach on

May 28, 1994.

The 213 feet high rollercoaster was built at a cost of £12 million and takes 3 minutes to ride at a maximum speed of 74mph.

On June 13, 1994

Nicole Brown, the estranged wife of American football star OJ Simpson and her friend Roland Goldman were found dead outside her condominium in Los Angeles.

Simpson, wanted in connection with their deaths, failed to turn himself in to the police but was spotted in his white bronco, driven by a friend on the Los Angeles interstate on June 17.

When approached by police, the driver, A.C. Cowlings, warned that OJ was in the back seat with a gun to his own head, threatening suicide.

A slow speed car chase commenced involving 20 police cars and 20 helicopters which lasted 45 minutes. It soon caught the attention of America's big television networks who broadcast the chase live, with an estimated 95 million viewers watching.

NBC continued their coverage of the NBA basketball finals, minimising the game between the New York Knicks and Houston Rockets to the corner of the screen with their main focus on the Simpson chase.

The chase ended at Simpson's home where he eventually turned himself in. He was charged with the murder of Brown and Goldman and in November 1994, a jury was sworn in for what would become, for the American media at least, the trial of the century commencing in January 1995.

June 15, 1994

saw the release of what is arguably the finest Disney movie ever made *The Lion King*.

Set in Africa and concerned with the life of a lion called Simba, *The Lion King* became an enormous hit, taking more than $772m at the box office from an original budget of just $45m. This made *The Lion King,* the most successful hand-drawn film and the most successful 2D animated film in cinema history.

It has since been re-released in 3D, and has now earned Disney more than $950m, and earned itself a place in the hearts of a generation.

LAW AND LIBERTY

A wide range of sweeping reforms were brought in by the **Criminal Justice and Public Order Act of 1994.** Introduced by the Conservative Home Secretary Michael Howard, this Act was not well received by civil liberties groups.

The Act tackled issues as wide-ranging as rights to silence, rights of police to stop and search, ticket touting, racially inflammatory material, obscene videos, obscene phone calls, copyright and illicit recordings.

Some of the most controversial aspects of the Act were featured in Part 5 dealing with Collective Trespass or Nuisance on Land. Opponents argued that this aspect of the Act was designed to suppress alternative culture in the legislation relating to travellers, squatters and the holding of raves.

The parts of the Act relating to raves caused much amusement for its definition of music as something that, "includes sounds wholly or predominantly characterised by the emission of a succession of repetitive beats".

Despite its reputation for the encroachment of civil liberties, one particularly liberalising aspect of the Act was its reduction of the age at which homosexual acts were lawful from twenty one years to eighteen.

July 6, 1994

saw the release of *Forrest Gump*, starring Tom
Hanks in a comedy drama which became the
top grossing film released in North America
that year. It was widely lauded by critics and
audiences alike, taking more than $677m
worldwide in 1994. More than that, it was
nominated for 13 Oscars, winning six, including
Best Picture, Best Actor for Tom Hanks and
Best Director for Robert Zemeckis.

**"Momma always said life was like
a box of chocolates. You never
know what you're gonna get."**

THE 1994 WORLD CUP

1994 saw the World Cup held in the United States of America; the first time that FIFA's showpiece event had taken place in the country. Organisers hoped that the World Cup would promote the sport in the USA, and the tournament was very successful in terms of attendances, with 3.6 million people attending the finals. It consisted of 24 teams divided into six groups of four, the last tournament before it was expanded to 32 teams in 1998. The tournament was won by Brazil, beating Italy in the July 17 final, on penalties after Roberto Baggio missed the crucial Italian penalty.

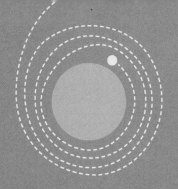

Excited Astronomers pointed their telescopes towards Jupiter for the Solar System's big event of the year in 1994 and they were not disappointed.

In March 1993, a very unusual comet called "Shoemaker Levy 9" (named from its discoverers) was identified. It was unusual because it was orbiting Jupiter, rather than the sun.

Astronomers calculated that it was captured by Jupiter from a solar orbit in the late 1960s or early 1970s and predicted it would collide with Jupiter in **July 1994.**

Their prediction was correct. From July 16 to July 22, fragments of the comet, some more than a mile in diameter, careered towards the planet at 37 miles per second.

They pounded the far side of the planet but the immediate impacts could be observed from the Galileo spacecraft. Since Jupiter rotates quite rapidly, the scars left by the impacts could be observed from earth within minutes.

In all there were 21 impacts leaving scars that could still be observed months later.

Tony Blair becomes Labour leader

July 21, 1994

saw Tony Blair become leader of the Labour Party after the death of John Smith. Blair was instrumental in galvanising the Labour Party, and reinventing it as "New Labour". Blair would sweep to power in a landslide in 1997, and spend a decade as Prime Minister, before being succeeded by his Chancellor, Gordon Brown.

SHOPPING ON SUNDAY

The Sunday Trading Act of 1994 considerably liberalised the rules surrounding Sunday trading. Prior to 1994, trading on Sunday was illegal, with a few exceptions as governed by the Shops Act of 1950.

In 1986, a parliamentary bill proposing wider Sunday trading was defeated, but The Sunday Trading Act which came into force on **August 28, 1994** made certain compromises.

Restrictions on Sunday opening hours enforced by the new Act apply mostly to larger stores of over 3,014 square feet where Sunday opening times are limited to no more than six hours, between 10am and 6pm.

August, 1994

saw the birth of Britpop, as Oasis released
their debut album *Definitely Maybe*. Containing
the singles "Supersonic", "Shakermaker",
"Live Forever" and "Cigarettes and Alcohol",
Definitely Maybe marked a rebirth for British
rock music, a shift away from the American
dominated Grunge scene, and a new
resurgence for rock and roll. Masterminded by
Noel Gallagher, with his brother Liam the band's
talismanic frontman, Oasis were about to
become the defining band of the next decade.

August 31, 1994

saw the **Provisional IRA** call a ceasefire,
declaring that from midnight there would be a,

"complete cessation of military operations"

The IRA called a ceasefire
on the basis that the political
wing of the organisation, Sinn
Fein, would be included in any
political discussions about
the future of Northern Ireland.
This did not happen, however,
with the British government
demanding that the IRA put
their weapons beyond use
before Sinn Fein would be
allowed to participate in any
political process. This lead to
the ceasefire being withdrawn
between 1996 and 1998, until
the signing of the Good Friday
Peace Accord on April 10,
1998, declared the war over.

UNIVERSITY CHALLENGE

University Challenge, which had been off British television screens since 1987, finally made a comeback in **September, 1994** with a new chairman. Jeremy Paxman took the chair previously occupied by Bamber Gascoigne, and set about giving a whole new generation of students their "starter for ten".

Fossil tree still alive and well and living in Australia

A species of tree previously only known through fossil records was discovered on **September 10, 1994** by David Noble a field officer at the Wollemi National Park in Wentworth Falls, New South Wales, Australia.

Named "Wollemia Nobilis", from its location and founder, the tree was previously only known through fossils throughout Australia dating back as many as 200 million years.

ALAN PARTRIDGE: KNOWING ME KNOWING YOU - AHA!

Fictional TV and radio presenter, Alan Partridge made his TV debut on **September, 16, 1994** in the BBC Television series *Knowing Me Knowing You*, his radio career having begun in 1992.

Partridge, depicted and created by Manchester comedian Steve Coogan is a narcissistic but rather insecure character obsessed with his own personal fame.

Knowing Me Knowing You ran to six episodes and was followed up by two seasons of a new series entitled *I'm Alan Partridge* featuring the man himself in 1997 and 2002.

September 19, 1994 saw the NBC, US, debut of *ER*.

The Chicago based medical drama became one of television's most popular shows, as well as launching the careers of actors such as George Clooney and Noah Wyle. Created by Michael Crichton, and based on his own experiences as a doctor in a busy emergency room, *ER*'s realism, drama, and humour had audiences hooked immediately, and they would stay that way for a fifteen season run which saw the show nominated for 375 awards, winning 115, including 22 Emmy Awards.

MICHAEL SCHUMACHER'S FIRST DRIVERS' CHAMPIONSHIP

1994 saw Michael Schumacher win his first Formula One Drivers Championship driving for Benetton, winning 8 of the races in which he took part. It was to be the first of seven Drivers Championships won by the German between 1994 and 2004, and the first Drivers' Championship ever won by a German.

September 22, 1994

saw the debut of one of the most successful
shows in television history –

F·R·I·E·N·D·S

It launched the careers of David Schwimmer, Courtney Cox,
Matthew Perry, Lisa Kudrow, Matt LeBlanc and Jennifer Aniston,
and became one of the most watched shows across the globe.
The show was so successful that by the ninth and tenth series
the actors were each being paid $1m per episode. When the
series finally ended in 2004 the finale episode was watched by
an incredible 51.1 million Americans.

....

**"I'll be there for you, (when the rain starts to fall)
I'll be there for you, (like I've been there before)
I'll be there for you,
'Cos you're there for me too."**

....

"FEAR CAN HOLD YOU PRISONER HOPE CAN SET YOU FREE"

The Shawshank Redemption, released **September 23, 1994** and based on a Stephen King novella is considered one of the best movies of the year, but made a rather modest impact at the time.

The movie features the story of a banker, played by Tim Robbins who is imprisoned, despite pleas of innocence, for the murder of his wife and her lover. It focuses on the prison friendship that develops between Robbins and a fellow inmate played by Morgan Freeman.

At the Box Office *The Shawshank Redemption* was overshadowed by *Pulp Fiction* and *Forrest Gump* and barely covered its costs. The Gump movie scooped several Academy Awards, leaving Shawshank with none.

The movie received greater recognition in subsequent years helped by Satellite and Cable broadcasts along with video and DVD sales. When The American Institute's 100 Years...100 Movies was first published in 1998, the movie did not feature, but in the same list of 2009 it outranked both *Forrest Gump* and *Pulp Fiction.*

"Suits you, Sir!"

September 27, 1994

saw the first episode of *The Fast Show*, the sketch show which redefined comedy for the 1990s.

In a sea-change for sketch shows, the first episode of *The Fast Show* featured twenty seven sketches in thirty minutes, relying·on recognisable characters, running gags and catchphrases, but setting itself apart from other catchphrase comedy shows by ensuring that they were used intelligently throughout the series. Featuring Paul Whitehouse, Charlie Higson, Simon Day, Mark Williams, John Thomson, Arabella Weir and Caroline Aherne, *The Fast Show* remains a firm favourite with British audiences.

The Premiership /
Manchester United won the title, finishing eight points ahead of Blackburn Rovers

The FA Cup /
Also won by Manchester United, making them the fourth team to achieve a league and cup double in the twentieth century (Tottenham in 1961, Arsenal in 1971 and Liverpool in 1986)

The Epsom Derby /
Won by Erhaab, ridden by Willie Carson

The Grand National /
Miinnehoma, ridden by Richard Dunwoody

Wimbledon Men's Singles Title /
Won by the American Pete Sampras, defeating Goran Ivanisevic in the final

Wimbledon Ladies' Singles Title /
A victory for Conchita Martinez, defeating the American Martina Navratilova

The County Championship /
Warwickshire, with Leicestershire second

The Five Nations Championship (Now the Rugby Union Six Nations) /
The first time the Championship was decided by points difference between the top two teams, giving Wales their 22nd title.

October 14, 1994

saw the US release of one of the biggest cult films of the '90s – **_Pulp Fiction._**

Directed by Quentin Tarantino and starring John Travolta as Vincent Vega and Samuel L. Jackson as Jules Winnfield, _Pulp Fiction_ follows the story of two mob hitmen who set out to recover a suitcase stolen from employer, Marsellus Wallace, played by Ving Rhames.

The movie features memorable performances from Uma Thurman, Rosanna Arquette and Bruce Willis as a boxer paid to throw a fight.

Tarantino and co-writer Roger Avary won an Oscar and BAFTA for Best Original Screenplay for _Pulp Fiction_ at the 67th Academy Awards, honouring the films of 1994. Most of the script had been written by the pair in Amsterdam during 1992.

Remarkably, the movie script had been turned down by TriStar who called it "demented and unfilmable".

Samuel L. Jackson picked up a BAFTA for Best Supporting role and the movie secured the coveted Palme d'Or Award at the 1994 Cannes Film Festival.

Irish boy band Boyzone first made their appearance on the UK chart in **1994**, with their cover of the Osmonds' "Love Me For A Reason" making its chart debut at number two. Boyzone were set to become one of the staples of the British pop charts in the 1990s, with a string of number 1 singles, number 1 albums, and over 20 million records sold worldwide.

Just because they serve you
doesn't mean they like you

Clerks, which came out in **October, 1994,** is the
first film by writer and director Kevin Smith, and
the first movie to be part of what has become
known as the "View Askewniverse". Shot over
21 days, entirely in black and white, and costing
just $27,575 to make, *Clerks* grossed over
$3m at the box office, launching Kevin Smith's
filmmaking career.

October 20, 1994,

The Guardian ran a story claiming that two Conservative Members of Parliament, Neil Hamilton and Tim Smith, had taken payments from Harrods owner Mohamed Al-Fayed to table parliamentary questions on his behalf, at a rate of £2000 per question. At the time Hamilton was a minister at the Department of Trade and Industry, whilst Smith was junior Northern Ireland minister. The two vehemently denied *The Guardian's* accusations, and writs of libel were issued against the paper. In 1996, just before the libel trial was due to begin, Hamilton withdrew his libel action, bringing condemnation from the press, and virtually ending his political career, as he was defeated in the 1997 election by Martin Bell running as an independent on an "anti-corruption" platform.

On November 5, 1994, a 45 year old George Foreman became the oldest ever heavyweight boxing champion.

Foreman regained the title he'd lost some twenty years earlier when he was defeated by Muhammad Ali on October 30, 1974.

Foreman's opponent on this occasion was Michael Moorer, 19 years his junior who outclassed, outpunched and outscored Foreman for nine rounds in this Las Vegas match.

In the tenth round Foreman, made a comeback, defeating Moorer with a knockout punch.

It was the longest interval that a boxer had ever waited to successfully regain a title and the biggest age gap between two heavyweight opponents.

The Richard Curtis created sitcom **The Vicar of Dibley** aired for the first time on British television on **November 10, 1994.**

The story, made plausible by the legalised ordination of women priests in the Church of England in 1992, features Dawn French in the title role as the Reverend Geraldine Chambers. In a later episode her full name is revealed as "Boadicea Geraldine Julie Andrews Dick Van Dyke Supercalifragilisticexpialidocious Chim Chiminey Chim Chiminey Chim Chim Cheree Granger".

Other regular characters featuring in the series included the rather conservative Parish Council chairman David Horton, his nice-but-dim son Hugo and the dippy Alice Tinker.

And the bonus ball is....

In a show hosted by Noel Edmonds, the first ever draw of the National Lottery took place on **November 19, 1994** with seven lucky jackpot winners sharing a prize of

£5,874,778.

The new lottery, licensed by Prime Minister John Major in 1993, is a state franchised lottery. The franchise was awarded to the Camelot group and is regulated by The National Lottery Commission.

The winning numbers for the first ever draw were:

3 5 14 22 30 44

Bonus Ball:

10

Laura Robson /
21 January 1994 / Australian born tennis player

Dakota Fanning /
23 February 1994 / American actress

Justin Bieber /
1 March 1994 / American pop star

Saoirse Ronan /
12 April 1994 / Irish actress

Mateo Kovacic /
6 May 1994 / Croatian football player

Tom Daley /
21 May 1994 / British diver

Deepika Prajapati /
13 June 1994 / Indian archer

Nyjah Huston /
30 November 1994 / American professional skateboarder

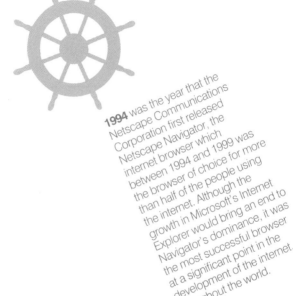

1994 was the year that the Netscape Communications Corporation first released Netscape Navigator, the internet browser which between 1994 and 1999 was the browser of choice for more than half of the people using the internet. Although the growth in Microsoft's Internet Explorer would bring an end to Navigator's dominance, it was the most successful browser at a significant point in the development of the internet, throughout the world.

TIME

Every year since 1927 TIME Magazine has produced a special issue that profiles someone they consider to be the person of the year.

The edition features a person, group, idea or object that for better or worse has done the most to influence the events of the year.

In 1981, the man of the year was Polish Solidarity leader Lech Walesa. Previous persons of the year have included Mohandas Gandhi (1930), Wallis Simpson (1936), Adolph Hitler (1938), Winston Churchill (1940), Elizabeth II (1952) and Ayatollah Khomeni (1979).

The 1994 TIME Magazine Man of the Year was ...

Pope John Paul II

5.602
BILLION

That's the number of people who lived in the world in 1994.

If you were around in 1994 apologies if we missed you out.

Just in case we did, here's the revised figure:

5.602 billion and **one** people lived in the world in 1994.